75 YEARS *of*
Children's
Book Week
Posters

75 Years of Children's Book Week Posters

CELEBRATING GREAT ILLUSTRATORS OF AMERICAN CHILDREN'S BOOKS

Sponsored by THE CHILDREN'S BOOK COUNCIL

With Introduction and Text by LEONARD S. MARCUS

ALFRED A. KNOPF : NEW YORK

THIS IS A BORZOI BOOK PUBLISHED BY ALFRED A. KNOPF, INC.

LIBRARY OF CONGRESS CATALOGING-IN-PUBLICATION DATA

75 years of children's book week posters / sponsored by the Children's Book Council; text by Leonard Marcus
p.   cm.
ISBN 0-679-85106-2 (trade)
[1. Children—United States—Books and reading—Posters. 2. Children's literature, American—Posters.
3. Posters, American.] I. Children's Book Council (New York, N.Y.)
Z1037.A1C465   1994   808.06'8—dc20   93-3692

Frontispiece: Children's Book Week poster by Jon O. Brubaker, 1925, 1926.
Manufactured in the United States of America
10 9 8 7 6 5 4 3 2 1

To John Donovan

The Children's Book Council would like to thank Carolyn Davis, at the Children's Literature Research Collection of the Walter Library in Minneapolis, and Lorraine Byrne, of the Westerly Public Library in Rhode Island, for their generous loan of posters to be photographed for this book.

Thanks are due to the following people and institutions for generous help with the research for this book: Jack Banning; Harriett Barton, creative director, HarperCollins Children's Books; Felicia Berg; Carol L. Birch, children's librarian, Chappaqua Library, Chappaqua, New York; Kit Breckenridge and Jill McConkey, the Free Library of Philadelphia; Donna Brooks, executive editor, Dutton Children's Books; Leslie Cabarga; Peter Carini, assistant archivist, Simmons College; Marcia Caspi; Caron Chapman, executive director, Association of Booksellers for Children; Margaret Coughlan, Children's Literature Center, the Library of Congress; Alva Cumming; Carolyn Y. Cummings, Boy Scouts of America; Dan Cupper; Paul Dobbs, archivist, Massachusetts College of Art; Connie Epstein; Andy Eskind, information technology manager, George Eastman House; James Fraser, chief librarian, Florham-Madison campus library, Fairleigh Dickinson University; Lillian N. Gerhardt, editor-in-chief, *School Library Journal*, Clarence Harnung; Susan Hirschman, editor-in-chief, Greenwillow Books; Poppy Johnson, children's librarian, Floyd Memorial Library, Greenport, New York; Dolores B. Jones, curator, the de Grummond Collection, University of Southern Mississippi; Amy Kellman, district coordinator, Children's Services, the Carnegie Library, Pittsburgh; Frank Lee; Anita Lobel; Ellen Loughran, coordinator, Public Service Support Office, Brooklyn Public Library; Anne Lows, Wolfsonian Foundation; Nancy MacKechnie, curator of rare books and manuscripts, Vassar College Library; Pat Magnani, Registrar's Office, Neuberger Museum of Art, State University of New York at Purchase; Tammy L. Martin, Oberlin College Archives; Emily Arnold McCully; Margaret K. McElderry, publisher, Margaret McElderry Books; James McMullan; Jean Mercier; Elena Millie, curator, poster collection, the Library of Congress; Angeline Moscatt and the staff of the Central Children's Room, the New York Public Library; Catherine O'Dea; Virginia O'Hara, curator, Brandywine Valley Museum; Jean Peters, librarian, Cahners Publishing Company; Bill Piper, Rand McNally Publishing Company; Paul Rand; Walt Reed; Charles Reibel; Joshua Reibel; Nathan Reibel; Ruth Reininghaus, chairman, curator's committee, Salmagundi Club; Jack Rennert; Diane Roback, children's book editor, *Publishers Weekly*; Norma Jean Sawicki, publisher, Ticknor & Fields Books for Young Readers; Richard Scarry; Terri Schmitz; Maurice Sendak; Uri Shulevitz; Rita Smith, the Baldwin Library, University of Florida at Gainesville; Sharyl G. Smith; Janet Somers, Westfield Memorial Library, Westfield, New Jersey; Jane Nichols Spragg; Susan Tolbert, the Smithsonian Institution; Elaine D. Trehub, archives librarian, Mount Holyoke College Library; Leonard Weisgard; Mus White; Paul O. Zelinsky; and Rebecca Zurier.

I wish also to express my appreciation to my editors, Janet Schulman and Maureen Sullivan, and to others on the staff of Knopf Books for Young Readers who contributed to the realization of this project; and to Paula Quint and the staff of the Children's Book Council.

Finally, to my wife and family I offer my heartfelt thanks for their encouragement, support, and love.

— L. S. M.

A Note from The Children's Book Council

The Children's Book Council, a nonprofit trade association promoting literacy and encouraging the reading and enjoyment of children's books, was created because children's book publishers recognized the importance of supporting National Children's Book Week, one of the first family-reading initiatives in America.

The basic concerns of making good books available to all young people and encouraging reading for enjoyment as well as instruction remain the cornerstone of the Council's work. The Council pursues this work through cooperative projects with major U.S. educational, library, and bookselling associations and by developing domestic and international programs that emphasize the importance of bringing literature to all children. In an increasingly less literate nation, this task is, perhaps, even more daunting now than it was in 1919, when Children's Book Week was inaugurated. It is a challenge I believe The Children's Book Council will continue to meet with imagination and energy.

Seventy-five years after its inception, Children's Book Week is still primary to our mission. It provides an annual opportunity to focus attention on how essential reading is to the intellectual and emotional lives of children, and it reminds us that we will have an informed adult citizenry only if we believe in and foster the importance of books and reading for our children.

Paula Quint
President

Introduction

"FRIENDS," warns the fast-talking flimflam artist of Meredith Willson's *The Music Man*. "Ya got trouble. Right here in River City!" It is 1912 in America's heartland, and the root of the fear that Willson's Professor Harold Hill deftly plays on lies not in the coming of pool to a prim and house-proud midwestern town but in the widely shared conviction of Americans of the time that theirs was an era of unprecedented, and potentially explosive, social change. Amid what many perceived as an impending breakdown of the traditional codes and customs of small-town community life, Americans pondered the impact of the new urban-generated values and influences then sweeping the nation, not just on their own way of life but on their children's moral welfare.

Americans at the start of the twentieth century were prospering as never before. But as the journalist Jacob A. Riis and others documented, large segments of the population—including significant numbers of children—were nonetheless living in abject circumstances. As reformers like Riis, Lincoln Steffens, and Jane Addams rose to combat the country's various social ills (not all of which affected only the lives of the poor), much of the idealism and emphasis focused on issues like infant nutrition, child labor practices, and public education—issues that related directly to the health and well-being of children.

It was in the context of this general outpouring of concern for the needs of the young that public libraries first experimented with establishing reading rooms for boys and girls toward the end of the nineteenth century. One purpose of creating the often delightful rooms, which by the 1910s were becoming a standard feature of libraries everywhere, was of course the fostering of an early love of books. Equally important, however, to the librarians who pioneered in this reform movement, was the earnest determination to monitor children's reading in an effort to shelter the young from premature exposure to the work of novelists like Balzac and (a bit later) Dreiser, whose piquant descriptions of the seamier aspects of life were deemed a vile threat to youthful morality. Also to be kept from innocent eyes were the supposedly lurid dime novels and series fiction published especially for the young, which featured shoot-'em-up plots, odious stock villains, and heroes so fantastically capable or lucky as to constitute rather dubious role models for youngsters. In an era when character-building was widely assumed to be the primary function of children's literature, librarians considered it their moral duty to offer the young "good" books while discouraging them from reading "trash." They hoped that parents would do the same. Between 1912 and 1915, the Boy Scouts of America, an organization dedicated to character-building, made it clear that they were prepared to do their part: the Scouts appointed Franklin K. Mathiews as their chief librarian; founded *Boys' Life* magazine ("strictly censored," as one advertisement stated, to eliminate all "harmful material"); issued an authoritative-sounding list of "Books Boys Like Best"; and experimented with the possibility of establishing some sort of annual week-long celebration of books and reading. In 1915, Mathiews decided to pursue this last idea beyond the bounds of the Scouting community with an all-

out national campaign that would harness the efforts of civic leaders, parents, teachers, librarians, newspaper and magazine editors, and others. Addressing the American Booksellers' Association that spring, the Scout Librarian declared in the high-toned, quasi-evangelistic manner of the day that bookshop owners were as morally duty-bound as librarians to help guide the nation's children in their reading habits. They too should be willing to take part in an annual juvenile book week.

Most booksellers of the time, it is safe to suppose, knew precious little about the juvenile trade. Shops specializing in children's books were rare. Most of those general-interest bookstores and department stores that carried children's titles did so only at year-end in time for Christmas gift-giving. Nonetheless, whether from hope or fear for the nation's future or merely in the reasonable expectation of profiting from such an event, Mathiews's audience rallied to the call for a Book Week observance. Planning proceeded slowly at first (and was tabled altogether during America's participation in World War I), but preparations began in earnest in the fall of 1918 for the following year's inaugural celebration. Mathiews early on had secured the wholehearted support of two powerful allies, the book industry trade journal's visionary editor, Frederic G. Melcher, and the New York Public Library's nationally known superintendent of children's work, Anne Carroll Moore. Both Melcher and Moore were vivid, forceful personalities and highly effective organizers. With their help, a Book Week Committee was formed with financial backing from the publishers' and booksellers' associations. One of the nation's most celebrated illustrators, Jessie Willcox Smith, was commissioned to design the official poster. Based on the slogan "More Books in the Home!," the poster would highlight parents' primary role in their children's moral education. The dates chosen for the first observance, November 10–15, 1919, fell strategically just before the start of the traditional holiday shopping season.

The Smith poster and a recommended-books list prepared by the committee were to be the campaign's centerpieces. Book Week events would be planned locally, however, with each city or town adapting the slogan theme (and, if desired, the list of program suggestions also supplied by the committee) to its own circumstances. The idea was to spark grass-roots interest in as many communities as possible, thereby laying the groundwork for a permanent, year-round commitment to books and reading. That first year, bookshops, libraries, and schools ordered 3,000 of the posters. Four years later, in 1923, orders had increased to 15,000, and the number would continue to climb.

Numerous contests in those first years offered children the chance to win "more books" by writing essays in praise of a favorite volume or by designing Book Week posters or bookplates or bookmarks of their own. Older boys were encouraged to build bookcases (which parents might then feel obliged to fill) and "add a shelf for every year," as the poster slogan for 1933 suggested outright. In some towns, parades featuring youngsters dressed as storybook characters beat a drum for the cause. Los Angeles

schoolchildren received cardboard "book banks" in which to save their pennies for whatever volume they most wanted to own. A York, Pennsylvania, furniture store converted its display window into a juvenile reading room where each day during Book Week a different handful of children spent their after-school hours in public view, browsing at books selected by the county librarian. In St. Louis, an automobile fitted with a library display toured the city's playgrounds, and in Boston, a bookshop dispatched its "caravan" each evening to heavily trafficked commuter rail stations, hoping to attract the attention of book-minded fathers.

Authors, illustrators, and the peripatetic Frederic G. Melcher addressed women's clubs, spoke at libraries, visited schools, and appeared at bookshops. Movie houses scheduled programs of films based on children's literature classics. *The New York Times* gave the campaign its blessing, as did the archbishop of Baltimore, James Cardinal Gibbons. Throughout the country, newspapers published suitably approving editorials, advice pieces by experts (usually librarians) on the wise and judicious selection of books for boys and girls, and reviews of the new season's offerings. "By dint of continuous publicity in women's magazines, in clubs and organizations of all kinds, it has become a common thing for mothers really to know and understand the problems of a diet for children," *The Publishers' Weekly* commented in October 1920 as the second annual observance drew near. "Is it not possible to make it equally the fashion to know about their intellectual diet?" The next year Bertha Mahony, manager of Boston's pioneering

Bookshop for Boys and Girls, restated one of the Book Week organizers' long-term goals when she predicted that the widespread interest the event had already generated would eventually extend "thruout [sic] the year."

Institutions critical to the attainment of that ambitious (and ultimately elusive) goal were just coming into being. Largely to satisfy the growing demand for books on the part of public libraries, Macmillan became in 1919 the first publisher to create a separate editorial department devoted to the production of books for young readers. Before that time, publishers had either imported juvenile books, taken on such books domestically on a haphazard basis, or relied on their collateral juvenile magazines (the most famous being Scribner's *St. Nicholas*) to originate material for compilation in book form. The new arrangement signaled a deepening commitment. By 1926, several leading trade houses—E. P. Dutton, Harper and Brothers, and Doubleday, Doran—had joined the field. Yet even as the new department heads (all of whom were women) were laying the foundation for a long-term symbiotic relationship with the nation's children's librarians, they found themselves struggling to maintain a certain status within their own firms. Book Week or not, the male managers of the major houses generally took a patronizing view of "juveniles." The pervasiveness of this attitude among publishers suggests the scope of the challenge that Melcher, Moore, and their colleagues faced in their attempts to educate the public.

Other important progress was nonetheless made.

The Newbery Medal, the first national prize for excellence in writing for children, was initiated in 1921. Melcher contributed both the idea and the funding for the annual award and in 1937 created a companion prize in illustration, the Caldecott Medal. Both prizes were administered by the American Library Association. In addition to providing authors and illustrators with a prestigious new form of recognition, the awards became the library establishment's ironclad assurance of quality to parents and others eager to provide children with the very best books.

In 1924, following a six-year stint as the juveniles reviewer for the monthly *Bookman,* the redoubtable Anne Carroll Moore undertook a weekly column in the pages of *The New York Herald-Tribune*. That same year, *The Horn Book* magazine, the field's first specialized review journal, began publication in Boston. In the nation's largest cities, shopping for the latest children's titles was even becoming a bit easier: During the prosperous 1920s, New York, Boston, Washington, D.C., San Francisco, and Los Angeles each boasted at least one children's-books-only bookstore. On the whole, however, booksellers either continued to exclude children's titles from their year-round inventories or to stock only a limited and often highly arbitrary selection, and few stores had staff knowledgeable enough to offer their customers much help.

The art poster, which first gained popularity in the United States in the late 1880s, rapidly established itself as a powerful expression, and symbol, of the nation's economic prosperity and cultural coming of age. Inspired by French and English examples, the first American posters advertised books and magazines. Soon equally striking graphics were touting the virtues of bicycles, patent medicines, even dynamite. The spectacular effectiveness of military recruitment posters during World War I (most notably James Montgomery Flagg's still-famous image of a resolute, star-spangled Uncle Sam) set an impressive standard for all sorts of planners of postwar advertising campaigns to emulate.

In Jessie Willcox Smith, the Book Week Committee had found its ideal artist. Mothers, it was assumed, were the principal audience to whom any appeal for "More Books in the Home!" had to be addressed. Smith's national prominence as *Good Housekeeping* magazine's regular cover artist assured the 1919 poster instant recognizability and cachet. The committee chose to reuse the design for the four following years; in 1925, when a new image was wanted, they again turned to Smith, while continuing to sound the clarion call for "More Books." For almost every year thereafter, a different artist and theme were chosen for the official poster.

Book Week slogans highlighted approved new trends in the literature or pointed up the timeliness of old standby books and their genres. In 1927, for example, works of "Romance, History, Travel"—including such spirited classics as Robert Louis Stevenson's *Treasure Island* (1883) and Howard Pyle's *The Merry Adventures of Robin Hood* (1883)—were featured in an effort to offset interest in the subliterary potboilers that the young continued, with

discouraging regularity, to read for thrills.

The 1931 theme "Round the World Book Fair" reflected American concern over the deepening turmoil in Europe. Unrest and unemployment abroad greatly exceeded parallel conditions in the United States; in Germany, the Weimar government was near collapse. Many books on publishers' lists that year offered the young a "real understanding of [the cultures of] other countries," as *The Publishers' Weekly* reported.

In the United States, the social fracturing caused by the Great Depression seemed to call forth a collective bid for reassurance that traditional values like Yankee ingenuity, stick-to-it-iveness, and the pioneering spirit still had some relevance. "Young America's Book Parade," the theme for 1932, put a cheerful face on the national soul-searching. Children's biographies of George Washington, Nathan Hale, Abraham Lincoln, and (most interestingly for the time) Harriet Tubman were published that fall, as was the first installment of Laura Ingalls Wilder's fictionalized account of her family's pioneer adventures, *Little House in the Big Woods*.

Some Book Week slogans suggested that fundamental changes in American cultural values had in fact been in the making for some time. Amid the astonishing (albeit turbulent) rise of the nation's modern industry-based, consumption-driven economy, the widely shared American mistrust of amusement and frivolity in the home and workplace—a legacy of Puritanism—was gradually dying. As psychologists expounded on the naturalness of humankind's pleasure-seeking impulses, a new army of copywriters and commercial artists contrived novel ways of channeling those impulses into a desire for consumable goods. On one level the call for "More Books in the Home!" merely echoed the appeals of countless national advertising campaigns for radios, soap suds, breakfast foods, and automobiles. (More often than not during the 1920s and 1930s, Book Week poster artists were drawn from the ranks not of children's illustrators but of commercial artists.)

Another significance of the shifting cultural climate was revealed in the dramatically altered emphasis of the critical debate about children's literature. In 1906, Clara Hunt of the Brooklyn Public Library spoke for many when she asserted that the "chief aim in the education of the child...is the *moral* aim....We claim for the children's library the possibility, the duty of being a moral force in the community." Each book a child read, Hunt declared, was sure to leave a lasting imprint for good or ill on the reader's soul. By the 1920s and 1930s, librarians were less concerned with molding children's souls than with stimulating their imaginations. It had become possible, if not obligatory, to advocate—as did the 1935 Book Week poster— "Reading for Fun."

During the Depression years, publishers sharply curtailed their children's lists. Some laid off staff or closed down their juvenile departments altogether. As though to underscore the mood of discouragement, the 1930 Book Week coincided with another promotional event called

Apple Week. An apple shippers' trade group had arranged to supply hundreds of unemployed Americans for a week with boxes of fruit to sell on street corners. The scheme generated so much favorable publicity that it was soon adopted year-round, furnishing the nation with one of its most bittersweet Depression-era memories. At year-end *The Publishers' Weekly* wondered only half in jest whether those dedicated to encouraging children's reading had missed an important opportunity by failing to devise a street-corner sales plan for books.

Throughout the Depression, interest in Book Week remained strong and continued to take new forms. Department stores around the country held elaborate book fairs that drew thousands of participants. Radio, reaching even larger numbers of people, played an increasingly vital part in the effort, as in daily life generally. From New York, for example, Alexander Woollcott broadcast his week-long Early Bookworm series of children's literature reviews over the Columbia Circuit. Eleanor Roosevelt lent her support in a magazine article. Grass-roots efforts also continued to spread, a touching instance of these efforts coming from the Midwest, where traveling libraries were started for rural children who had no access to books apart from their school texts. Estimates for 1934 indicated that 10,000 schools had planned projects around the event, over 5,000 libraries had installed special displays, and more than 500 local civic groups had devoted their November meetings to the discussion of children's reading.

By 1935, the American economy had improved

somewhat. With their skills honed on adversity, publishers cautiously began to expand their children's lists again. The legacy of this period would consist above all in an abundance of memorable picture books: Munro Leaf and Robert Lawson's *The Story of Ferdinand* (1936); Ludwig Bemelmans's *Madeline* (1939); Ingri and Edgar Parin d'Aulaire's *Abraham Lincoln* (1939); Margaret Wise Brown and Leonard Weisgard's *The Noisy Book* (1939); Virginia Lee Burton's *Mike Mulligan and His Steam Shovel* (1939); Robert McCloskey's *Make Way for Ducklings* (1941); H. A. Rey's *Curious George* (1941); Margaret Wise Brown and Clement Hurd's *The Runaway Bunny* (1942); and many others. That the Book Week posters of the period reflect so little of this extraordinary burst of creativity cannot but disappoint; these posters, however, are of particular interest for another reason. Those for 1938 through 1942 are cast in the boldly contemporary visual idiom that Americans had come to associate with the community-minded public-service "people's art" of the WPA. As such, the posters of these years were the first to present Book Week in a larger societal context, claiming for children's books an important role not just in the home but in the life of the nation.

Soon after the United States entered World War II, Frederic Melcher expressed concern that the hard-won progress of the advocates of children's reading might be lost under the "strain of wartime living." Americans, he wrote in *The Publishers' Weekly,* needed to realize that the future of a democracy ultimately depended on its citizens' ability to read well and think clearly. Adults who had not mastered these skills as children were not likely to acquire them later. Book Week, Melcher wrote, ought thus to be viewed as an essential element of the war effort. "Build the Future with Books," as the poster for 1943 urged.

To the surprise of many, the war years proved to be a boom time for children's publishing. War industry centers around the country provided nursery schools where children and their working parents were exposed, often for the first time, to picture books and the pleasures of reading. With steel for bicycles, rubber for balls, and other materials in even shorter supply than paper and binding materials, Americans turned to books as gifts of choice for their youngsters. Surveying the gratifying trend, Melcher concluded that parents by the thousands had simply realized that books were "among the things" they most wanted to "see their children have in greater abundance."

As history books and fictional tales of heroism offered children of the period a vicarious sense of participation in the war effort, librarians and publishers debated the extent to which books for the young should report frankly on the terrifying realities of the war itself. A consensus emerged that children below the age of six were better spared any detailed knowledge of the fighting (though one wonders how in the radio age and with fathers in virtually every community away at the front this could have seemed possible). F. Hasse's poster for 1942 had to be repainted to eliminate the frightening specter of an enemy plane being shot down over a city that was itself in flames. Elizabeth Orton Jones's poster for the following year presented no such difficulties. Jones's sunny depiction of an all-American country lad, a sort of book-minded Tom Sawyer, bore a striking resemblance, as it happened, to the hero of Robert McCloskey's *Homer Price* of that same year—a storybook widely hailed at the time as a summing up of everything the nation was fighting to preserve.

Looking back over the thirty years of his career in the fall of 1943, Frederic Melcher noted with pride that children's book publishing had grown from exceedingly modest beginnings to constitute "almost a separate industry." The handful of firms that had maintained children's editorial departments during the 1920s had increased to about fifty publishers, and twice that number published children's books occasionally. In 1944, representatives of thirty publishers met to found the Association of Children's Book Editors. The Association in turn established the Children's Book Council to administer Book Week and to serve as a clearinghouse for information about the field, which was certain to expand after the war.

In the years following World War II, American graphic art became less assertively monumental, more relaxed and even playful in tone and outlook. Images were less apt to tower or march in pictorial space: The new images floated, hovered, and gave the unmistakable impression that whoever made them had been having a good time. The d'Aulaires' heroic Book Week poster for 1947 and Lynd Ward's impas-

sive 1954 design belonged to an earlier age. More typical of the changed attitude in graphics were Elizabeth Tyler Wolcott's elegant (but disarmingly casual) poster for 1949 and Jan Balet's winsome interpretation in 1953 (reminiscent of the women's fashion magazine covers of the period) of three impish sophisticates deployed in and around a contemporary butterfly chair. The new art suited a nation that had defeated totalitarianism abroad, preserved its own democratic way of life, and moved to the suburbs.

The postwar baby boom caused publishers to expand their juvenile lists, especially in the area of books for the younger ages. Margaret Wise Brown and Clement Hurd's quintessential bedtime book, *Goodnight Moon,* was published in 1947. Robert McCloskey's *One Morning in Maine* (1952) celebrated the simple pleasures of close-knit family living. Ruth Krauss's *The Carrot Seed* (1945), illustrated by her husband, cartoonist Crockett Johnson, and Dr. Seuss's *If I Ran the Zoo* (1950) showed both the good and the fun that could come of encouraging the young—as progressive educators and others had been advocating for decades—to trust their imaginative impulses and to think for themselves. The Book Week posters for these years—those, for example, by William Pène du Bois, Roger Duvoisin, and Garth Williams—attest to a new depth in the pool of artists who were choosing to make children's book illustration an important part of their lifework.

Parents eager to provide their children with a home library had in some respects never had an easier time of it. A variety of new book clubs made it possible to purchase books by mail and for school-aged children to make their own selections, under a teacher's watchful eye, in the classroom. An innovative publishing venture begun during the war—Simon and Schuster's Golden Books imprint—conveniently offered its picture books for sale from racks in five-and-dime stores and drugstores, and for a fraction of the price of the traditional trade titles that could only be found (if they *could* be found) in bookstores. Librarian-critics like Anne Carroll Moore scoffed at the trim, bright tinsel-bound storybooks as the literary equivalent of canned vegetables. People bought them anyway, by the hundreds of thousands, which is to say in vastly larger quantities than the traditional publishers had ever been able to sell theirs. Not surprisingly, ambitious, talented authors and illustrators found it worth their while to work for Simon and Schuster (and after 1958 for the Golden Press), and some very good books were the outcome. Among the Book Week poster artists who contributed to the early Golden Books lists were Leonard Weisgard, Garth Williams, Alice and Martin Provensen, and Feodor Rojankovsky.

Although older houses like Dutton, Doubleday, and Harper never quite conceded the retail side of the business to the publishers of Golden Books and their imitators, they tended throughout the 1950s and beyond to focus primarily on their profitable relationship with their library friends. Postwar prosperity strengthened those ties even as most booksellers continued to ignore a specialty they considered bothersome. If children wished to experience the "fun" of reading, as the 1952 Book Week poster implied, they might

consider visiting their local library.

With an association to back them and with rising profits to show for their labors, children's book editors were feeling confident as never before. Book Week in those years opened with a gala banquet in the grand ballroom of New York's Astor Hotel. Around the country, big-city book fairs, typically sponsored by a major newspaper in association with the Children's Book Council and hosted by a local museum, gained in popularity. In 1953, fairs were held in New York, Washington, D.C., Cleveland, Detroit, Little Rock, and Chicago, where 48,000 people filed into the Museum of Science and Industry to view the book displays and meet such notable authors and illustrators as Lynd Ward, Don Freeman, and the d'Aulaires. That same year, the new medium of television, soon to become the most controversial factor in the equation for everyone dedicated to bringing children and books together, was briefly enlisted in the cause when the Ford Foundation–sponsored program *Excursion* featured a half-hour of Book Week readings and commentary by Burgess Meredith, Helen Hayes, and Raymond Massey. For a week, children's books were also a topic on the *Howdy Doody* show and Dave Garroway's *Today Show*. In past years, mayors and governors had issued proclamations lending the prestige of their offices to the validation of Book Week's worthy goals. In 1953, for the first time, the president of the United States did so as well.

A new arrival on the early-fifties publishing scene, Ann Durrell, later recalled the Eisenhower years as an

"Indian summer," when publishing, like American society generally, was "dominated by a sort of mid-Atlantic bourgeoisie that felt it had saved the world for democracy and had thus earned the right to perpetuate forever the sociological and cultural values of Edwardian England."

The *My Fair Lady*–like serenity of the period was, however, easily shattered. Rudolf Flesch's 1955 bestseller *Why Johnny Can't Read* accused the nation's schools of having failed to teach basic literacy skills to large numbers of children. Then in 1957, the launching of *Sputnik I* touched off new fears that the nation had fallen dangerously behind its Soviet nemesis in scientific research and science education for its children.

Although their efforts went largely unheralded at the time, children's book publishers responded constructively to both these calls to action. From Random House came Dr. Seuss's *The Cat in the Hat* (1957), the first in the Beginner Books series intended to supplant the sodden adventures of Dick and Jane with storybooks children might really enjoy while learning to read. Harper's competing I Can Read series made an equally auspicious debut with the publication of Else Holmelund Minarik's *Little Bear* (1957), illustrated by Maurice Sendak. When the National Defense Education Act of 1958 provided federal funds for the library purchase of children's books on science and mathematics, a profusion of new titles in these fields appeared in response.

Then in 1959, the publication of Garth Williams's *The Rabbits' Wedding,* a picture book in which a white rabbit and a black rabbit marry, was met with an hysterical wave of book bannings and threatened book burnings in the segregationist South. The controversy surrounding the book received worldwide press coverage and reflected the increasingly volatile state of American race relations following the 1954 *Brown* v. *Board of Education* decision and the forced desegregation of the Little Rock public schools three years later. By the end of the decade, some publishers were beginning to question the adequacy, and moral efficacy, of what critic Nancy Larrick, writing in the *Saturday Review,* would condemn as the "all-white world of children's books." Adrienne Adams's Book Week poster for 1963 was the first to include the image of an African-American child.

That same year Maurice Sendak's *Where the Wild Things Are* broke new ground as it violated the unwritten taboo against picture-book children talking back to their parents—or expressing their rage. Other stereotypes of childhood innocence were challenged with the publication of *Harriet the Spy* (1964), Louise Fitzhugh's novel about an edgy, headstrong, imaginative eleven-year-old girl who habitually sneaks into her neighbors' homes to keep tabs on their activities. Just as unprecedented (some at the time said scandalous) were Harriet's cocktail-drinking parents, who take Harriet in for a friendly chat with a therapist when they can no longer cope with her themselves. Novelist John Donovan and picture-book artists Ezra Jack Keats and Tomi Ungerer (the latter of whom became as famous during the 1960s for his antiwar posters as for his wickedly amusing children's fables) were among the decade's other pathfinders. As rebels, however, they remained a distinct minority within their field. When Emily Arnold McCully's 1969 Book Week poster appeared, featuring a gingerly depiction of youngsters "demonstrating" for "Book Power," hundreds of angry letters from teachers and librarians poured into the Children's Book Council office, questioning the appropriateness of the image. The next year's poster, treading ever more lightly, proposed that if the Age of Aquarius had arrived, so too perhaps had the "Age of the Book." The joke must have gone over well enough: The following year's poster brightly proclaimed a "Read-In."

As part of the Johnson administration's Great Society, Congress had appropriated vast sums of federal money for the purchase of nontextbooks for school and public libraries. Ann Durrell, who by then had become children's editor at Holt, Rinehart and Winston, recalled that as long as this "golden largess" lasted, "sales were such that publishers could afford almost anything that they or their authors or illustrators wanted in the way of book production. Lavish full-color books printed on thick beautiful paper, with bindings reinforced for library use, began to appear. . . . Excellence in design became a competitive goal. . . . Artists were able to experiment with every facet of their creative powers." By the end of the decade, the impressive profits that resulted from this surge made publishers with strong children's lists look attractive as takeover targets for corporations eager to diversify their interests. The trend toward mergers and acquisitions begun at this time was to continue, and dramatically accelerate,

into the 1980s and 1990s, while also becoming, like publishing itself, increasingly international in scope.

With the greatly expanded number of school libraries made possible by Johnson-era funding came new opportunities for Book Week observances. Recognizing bookseller indifference, the Children's Book Council concentrated its efforts on the libraries and schools, and few school-aged children got through the month of November without the special experience of some reading or story-telling event, author appearance, or visit to one of the many local book fairs that the Council sponsored in communities beyond the range of the still-flourishing major city fairs.

A growing assortment of visual aids was being offered to help mark the occasion and to preserve for year-round use in brightening institutional ceilings and walls. In 1968, for example, the Council produced not only Ellen Raskin's poster but also a mobile by Anne Rockwell and decorative streamers by Anita Lobel, Harriet Pincus, and cartoonist Charles M. Schulz. (Schulz's designs featured captions in Russian and Spanish as well as English.) Perhaps the greatest single visual aid to literacy of this time, however, came from another, unexpected source—television. Starting in 1969, children had something remarkable to view: Public Television's *Sesame Street,* which along with much else blithely taught the young their ABC's.

By the mid-1970s, however, the Nixon administration had terminated federal funding for children's book purchases, and publishers, once more finding themselves overextended, were forced to cut back their departments and their lists. Libraries saw their staffs and budgets decimated, and as inflation spiraled toward the end of the decade, the situation only worsened.

Offsetting somewhat the publishers' difficulties was the success of an experiment undertaken by several houses for the first time to bring out a variety of children's books in paperback—books inexpensive enough for youngsters to purchase themselves. Librarians, with their long tradition of the aesthetically uplifting "book beautiful," had always shunned them. Children, it turned out, often preferred paperbacks. Sales soared. Eventually, libraries began to purchase paperbacks too.

Many of the new books were novels that frankly addressed questions about sexuality, drug use, the home life of families fractured by divorce, and other formerly unmentionable subjects that had now become impossible to ignore. As the period of the so-called "problem novel" continued into the 1970s, the boundary separating children's books from the rest of literature seemed to blur. Strikingly, books for the younger ages gravitated toward the opposite extreme of the "timeless" fairy tale and fable. There was doubtless an element of the old protective attitude toward the young in this trend, though as Bruno Bettelheim argued in his influential *The Uses of Enchantment* (1976), the real significance of fairy tales perhaps lay not in their escapist, never-never-land aspect but rather in their incomparable power to convey hard psychological truths in irreducibly clear symbolic form. Several of the artists chosen to design Book Week posters during the 1970s either specialized, like

Margot Zemach, in illustrating retellings of traditional stories or, like William Steig and James Marshall, were known for their original picture-book fables. In the post-Watergate era of moral cynicism and societal drift, these wry, canny artists brought home truths that the young might realistically embrace while learning to laugh at life's absurdities.

Then dramatic developments first observed in the late 1970s once again utterly transformed the scene. The children of the postwar baby boom were coming of age. Many were college-educated and had postponed marriage while establishing themselves professionally. When at last they formed families of their own, they brought to the experience of parenthood a keen respect for learning, vibrant memories of certain childhood books they had loved, and, very often, the money with which to provide their own children with the best books publishers had to offer. As consumers, they prodded their local booksellers to accommodate their families' needs, and more than a few booksellers responded by making room for an adequate children's section in their stores. At the same time, former children's librarians around the country, some of them motivated by longstanding personal commitments to social activism, were deciding on a once-unthinkable alternative for women of their training and going into business, opening bookshops that either emphasized or were devoted entirely to children's literature. In 1973, a half dozen such specialty stores existed in the United States. Ten years later, there were two hundred of them and by 1993 twice that number had opened their doors.

Publishers responded to the intense new demand—not only from parents but also from teachers looking for refreshing nontextbook supplements to their grade-school curricula—by publishing many more children's books than ever. More publishers entered the field, while those already established in it were compelled to acknowledge as never before the vital importance of their children's departments to their overall operation. As sales in the retail market for books overtook the library market, different kinds of books were introduced or emphasized. More books for babies and toddlers appeared. Nonfiction books of all sorts shed their traditionally dreary institutional skin and became eye-catchingly marketable. As educators extolled the virtues of reading aloud to one's children from infancy (if not, as a few even suggested, in utero), picture books (always a popular genre) glutted the stores. The Book Week posters of the 1980s and early 1990s suggest, but come nowhere near to exhausting, the extraordinary range of talented artists who had come to work in the field.

Books also began to reflect more accurately the actual makeup of American society. In 1980, for example, books representing the cultural background and experiences of African-American children had little more than a token presence within the literature. By the early 1990s, a splendid library of such books was available. Bilingual books, a sustained interest in which had been pioneered by some of the hundreds of "alternative" presses that sprouted in the United States and Canada, also found a place in the mainstream, as did books on a wide range of difficult or

formerly taboo subjects such as death and bereavement, homelessness, and AIDS.

At the same time, however, the children's book world had become increasingly subject to faddish trends and to more deep-seated commercial pressures. In the new publishing environment brought on by two decades of corporate takeovers and consolidations, more books were published primarily because publishers knew they could market the books effectively rather than because they believed that children would want them. Picture books by celebrities epitomized the trend; and in an effort to capture the attention of the legions of untutored parents wandering into bookshops—and the cavernous new superstores—around the country, picture books, generally, became larger in format and splashier in design. Taking the centuries-old tradition of the children's novelty book to new levels of sophistication (and more than occasionally of mindless gimmickry), some books also popped out fetchingly at the would-be customer or made assertive chirping sounds or came packaged with a plush toy or locket or plastic bug. While a few books earned previously unimaginable sums for their authors, illustrators, and publishers, those that failed to quickly find their audience were more apt than before, in the stately, deliberative library-dominated years, to be unceremoniously dropped from the lists. Children's publishing—total sales of which skyrocketed from $475 million in 1985 to over $1 billion just six years later—had begun to resemble the high-stakes, rough-and-tumble world of publishing for grownups. Few veterans of the hard-won battles of the past could contemplate the astonishing spectacle of the field's newfound success without mixed emotions.

As the seventy-fifth anniversary of Book Week approached, Americans, it seemed clear enough, had yet to become a nation of readers. Public libraries had been left to founder in a shameful condition of financial and spiritual disarray. The commercial mass media, while always prepared to decry the substandard reading levels of the nation's schoolchildren, had little airtime or print space to spare for a thoughtful discussion of the very books which, if only more people knew about them, might make lifelong readers of countless youngsters.

Yet there can be little doubt that the Book Week founders would have marveled at some of the new resources and vastly changed circumstances that defined the American children's book scene of the early 1990s. An impressive variety of books had at last become available year-round in large numbers of stores. Many of these books were also in continual use in school classrooms and could even be met at home through innovative programs like the PBS television show *Reading Rainbow*. At the same time, nonprofit organizations like Reading Is Fundamental were making a concerted effort to distribute books to children who could not otherwise afford to have any books of their own.

Would Americans decide, with Frederic Melcher, that children's reading was "everyone's concern," not a frill of childhood but a matter of central importance to the future of our own, or any, democratic society? It remained to be seen. Meanwhile, these posters offer us an absorbing view of seventy-five years of American illustration art and design, and of our nation's changing attitude toward children's books and toward the people for whom children's books are made.

— Leonard S. Marcus

75 YEARS *of* Children's Book Week Posters

1919-1923 and 1930

JESSIE WILLCOX SMITH
(1863–1935)

Smith was born in Philadelphia and studied with Thomas Eakins at the Pennsylvania Academy of the Fine Arts. Her most important teacher, however, was Howard Pyle, the master illustrator who helped launch not only Smith's pathfinding career as a woman in the arts but also those of her two closest professional friends, Elizabeth Shippen Green and Violet Oakley. Another formative influence that Smith acknowledged were the prints and paintings of American expatriate Mary Cassatt.

One of the most successful illustrators of her day, Smith was especially well known for her poignant, richly colored depictions of mothers and their children. Among the popular children's books she illustrated are Mabel Humphrey's The Book of the Child *(1903), Robert Louis Stevenson's* A Child's Garden of Verses *(1905), and* The Jessie Willcox Smith Mother Goose *(1914). But it was as a cover artist for* Good Housekeeping *and* Collier's *magazines that Smith doubtless reached her largest audience. At the time Smith was asked to design the first Book Week poster, her work was instantly recognizable to millions of Americans.*

1924

Jessie Willcox Smith
(1863–1935)

Smith drew the cover illustration for every issue of Good Housekeeping *from December 1917 through April 1933—an astonishingly long run. On introducing her to the magazine's readers, the editors praised Smith's work as representing "the highest ideals of the American home, the home with that certain wholeness one associates with a sunny living room—and children."*

1925, 1926

Jon O. Brubaker
(1875–date unknown)

Little is known of the work of this apparently remarkable graphic artist, who was born in Dixon, Illinois, and later lived in Greenport, New York. Brubaker studied with George B. Bridgman at the Art Students League and at the Académie Julien, in Paris, and seems to have begun his career as a landscape painter. In the early 1920s, Brubaker shifted his focus to commercial art. Writing in the trade journal The Poster *in February 1925, he observed: "Five years ago I could not have been convinced that advertising posters were in any way artistic, but today. . . I am convinced that Poster Advertising has been a contributing factor to bringing Art to the people."*

During the 1920s, Brubaker earned a considerable reputation as a railroad poster artist. He also produced numerous promotional pieces for the outdoor advertising service of O. J. Gude. He was a member of the Artists Guild, and in 1926, the Art Directors Club awarded him its gold medal in poster design for the Book Week poster shown here.

BOOKS

ROMANCE HISTORY TRAVEL

N.C.W.

N. C. WYETH
(1882–1945)

The favorite student of Howard Pyle and patriarch of America's most celebrated artistic dynasty, N. C. Wyeth was among the most accomplished and prolific illustrators of his generation. Wyeth executed numerous large murals, still lifes and landscape paintings, and posters for such clients as Coca-Cola, the Pennsylvania Railroad, and the American Red Cross. His first love, however, was book illustration, and by 1927, when his Book Week poster was first issued, Wyeth had already completed many of the zestful commissions for which he is still known. Among these are the Scribner's Illustrated Classics editions of Robert Louis Stevenson's Treasure Island *(1911) and* Kidnapped *(1913) and James Fenimore Cooper's* The Deerslayer *(1925).*

The slogan "Romance History Travel" was intended to highlight three genres of literature that parents might introduce their children to in the reasonable expectation of weaning them away from such "trashy"—but nonetheless popular—varieties of juvenile reading matter as the dime novel and Sunday comics. If any American artist was well qualified to tout the virtues of the literature of history, travel, and high romance, it was Newell Convers Wyeth.

ROBERT C. GELLERT
(DATES UNKNOWN)

As a well-respected commercial artist, Gellert designed advertisements for Gulf Oil, Sanka coffee, the Abraham & Straus department store, and other corporate clients. In 1930, he received the Art Directors Club's gold medal for best poster of the year for a design he created for Atwater Kent, a manufacturer of radios.

The open, rhythmic design of Gellert's Book Week poster and his choice of bold, rounded type suggest the influence of such European masters of avant-garde poster design as Ludwig Hohlwein and Lucian Bernhard (the latter of whom had left Germany in 1923 and established a practice in New York), though Gellert's treatment of his subject is ultimately more restrained.

8

1931

MAUD PETERSHAM
(1889–1971) AND
MISKA PETERSHAM
(1888–1960)

During the 1920s and 1930s, the period of their greatest activity, the Petershams were among the children's book world's most admired figures. Miska, a Hungarian émigré, and Maud, a rural northeasterner and Vassar graduate, had met in New York as young commercial artists. Their first collaborations in book illustration included work for classics by Charles and Mary Lamb and Washington Irving, and a new book destined to become a classic, Carl Sandburg's Rootabaga Stories *(1922). Like Sandburg's phantasmagorical yarns, the Petershams' art was an eclectic brew of folk and modernist ingredients. In the Petershams' case, the folk influence was largely Hungarian in origin. Their illustrations for Margery Clark's* The Poppy Seed Cakes *(1924) and for their own* Miki *(1929) and* The Ark of Father Noah and Mother Noah *(1930) are among their best.*

YOUNG AMERICA'S BOOK PARADE

WALTER COLE
(1891–DATE UNKNOWN)

Born in New York City, Cole studied drawing under George B. Bridgman at the Art Students League. A well-regarded figure in the New York commercial art world of the 1930s and 1940s, Cole was primarily known as a line artist specializing in scratchboard, a drawing technique that, in reproduction, gives the effect of a woodcut or engraving. His advertising clients included the Sinclair Refining Company, General Electric, and Coca-Cola. His only book for children, A B C Book of People, was published in the same year as this poster.

Chosen to complement the previous year's theme, which emphasized books about foreign peoples and places, the 1932 slogan presented opportunities to feature juveniles with unabashedly patriotic, American themes. In that Depression year, such books were in ample supply; perhaps the best of the lot was one published in the fall, Laura Ingalls Wilder's Little House in the Big Woods.

1933

Ruth Alexander Nichols
(1893–1970)

A nationally known commercial photographer, Nichols was born in Bethany, Nebraska, and raised in Hiawatha, Kansas, where, at the age of nine, she won her first box camera in a magazine contest. On graduating from Oberlin College, she freelanced, married, and started a family. A two-page spread in the November 1925 issue of Good Housekeeping, *consisting of snapshots of her own two-year-old daughter, established Nichols's reputation as an adept photographer of child subjects. Johnson & Johnson, the Prudential Insurance Company, and Steinway & Sons, the piano manufacturer, were among the many corporate clients who enlisted her services for their advertising.* Collier's, McCall's, National Geographic, *and* Life *all featured her photographs of boys and girls.*

In the early 1930s, photography was a largely untried medium of children's book illustration. Wary critics feared that the uncompromising realism of photographs might blunt children's creativity. Nonetheless, riding the wave of enthusiasm generated by the publication of Edward Steichen and Mary Steichen Martin's landmark First Picture Book: Everyday Things for Babies *(1930), Nichols herself produced a series of photographically illustrated books for young readers, starting with* Nancy *(1933) and* Billy *(1934).*

GRACE A. PAULL
(1898–1990)

Born in Cold Brook, New York, Paull trained with Alexander Archipenko, George B. Bridgman, and George C. Miller. She designed greeting cards before entering the children's book field, where she quickly established herself with her buoyantly self-assured comic style of illustration. Among her early works were such well-received storybooks as Margery Bianco's A Street of Little Shops *(1932) and* The Good Friends *(1934). Paull went on to illustrate dozens more, including books by Eliza Orne White, Carolyn Sherwin Bailey, Elizabeth Coatsworth, and Clyde Robert Bulla.* Four Friends *(1935) was the first of more than a dozen children's books that she both wrote and illustrated.*

1935

RICHARD FLOETHE
(1901–1992)

Born in Essen, Germany, and trained at the Bauhaus, Floethe came to the United States in the early 1930s, pursuing a dual career in book illustration and poster design. To the children's book world, he became best known as the illustrator of Noel Streatfeild's Ballet Shoes *(1937) and its many sequels. From 1936 to 1939, as administrator and art director of the New York City Federal Art Project's poster division, Floethe created innovative, Bauhaus-inspired posters while overseeing the output of a large and bustling studio of designers. For his Book Week poster, however, Floethe eschewed modernism in favor of a quaint, anecdotal style.*

1936

JAY MAURICE REIBEL
(1888–1962)

This able commercial artist worked at various times for himself, in industry, and for two of the nation's largest advertising agencies. Reibel was four when his family immigrated from Europe to the United States, settling in Elizabeth, New Jersey. As a young man, he enrolled in the Art Students League, where he studied under George B. Bridgman and William Merritt Chase. During the 1920s, Reibel joined the J. Walter Thompson agency, later moving to McCann–Erickson, where he was assigned to the firm's Berlin and Paris offices. He returned to New York in 1932 to found his own agency, with Marlboro cigarettes as his major account; it was during this period of his career that Reibel designed the poster seen here. In later years, he headed the advertising department of the American Car and Foundry Company, manufacturers of railroad rolling stock and, during World War II, of armaments.

KENNETH S. FAGG
(1901–1980)

A versatile commercial artist, Fagg worked as an art director for Fox Films during the 1920s and later contributed illustrations for Life *and* Holiday *magazines. The artist, whose fascination with aerial perspectives led him to do much of his research from airborne planes, also illustrated science fiction books. At the time he produced "The Magic Highway to Adventure," Fagg was co-owner of Geo-Physical Maps, Inc., a firm that made globes of the planets.*

1938

JOSEPH BINDER
(1898–1972)

This influential artist's career spanned the avant-garde experiments in poster design of 1920s Vienna and America's rather reluctant embrace during the following decades of similarly bold, nontraditional approaches to graphic art and design. Born in Austria and trained as a painter at Vienna's State School of Arts and Crafts, Binder achieved early international success as a poster artist. During the early 1930s, he toured the United States as a visiting lecturer. At a time when American graphic art had largely become stalled in a guarded style of anecdotal realism, Binder's spirited advocacy of machine-age modernism did much to improve the climate for innovation. In 1935, he moved permanently to New York, where exhibitions of his work and important commissions followed. Binder won the coveted assignment of creating the official poster for the 1939 New York World's Fair. In 1941, he received both first and second prize in a poster competition sponsored by the Museum of Modern Art. Fortune magazine, Ballantine Beer, the U.S. Army Air Corps, and the American Red Cross were among his clients. In later years, Binder increasingly devoted himself to painting in the non-objective, minimalist style he considered the ultimate refinement in his lifelong search for the essential elements of visual communication.

1939

RALPH BELL FULLER
(DATES UNKNOWN)

As a graphic artist, Fuller appears to have taken his lead from the work of such contemporary masters of poster design as Joseph Binder.

The 1939 Book Week slogan was an obvious, if ultimately ironic, choice for the year that began in high anticipation of the opening of the New York World's Fair, with its vision of international cooperation and the triumph of modern technology, and that ended with Germany's invasion of Poland and the outbreak of war in Europe.

BOOK WEEK
NOVEMBER 10 TO 16

GOOD BOOKS GOOD FRIENDS

MAUD PETERSHAM
(1889–1971) AND
MISKA PETERSHAM
(1888–1960)

*The heroic stridency of the Petershams' 1940
poster design suggests a familiarity with the
propagandistic imagery emanating from the
Soviet Union and Germany. Such militancy
was a striking departure for them—and one
with which, to judge by the stiffness of the
design, they plainly felt uncomfortable. The
artists had become deeply concerned about
the deteriorating world situation. Their next
two books,* An American ABC, *which was a
1942 Caldecott Honor winner, and* The
Rooster Crows: A Book of American
Rhymes and Jingles, *which won the 1946
Caldecott Medal, were both devoted to patriotic themes.*

1941

HELEN SEWELL
(1896–1957)

*Like Grace A. Paull (1934), with whom she shared a studio for a time in New York, Sewell studied with Alexander Archipenko. Her formally rigorous (but generally light-hearted) approach to illustration seems at times almost as closely related to sculpture as to drawing. Sewell never stopped experimenting: each of her picture books—*A B C for Every Day *(1930),* Ming and Mehitable *(1936), and* Jimmy and Jemima *(1940), as well as her illustrations for Langston Hughes's* The Dream Keeper and Other Poems *(1932)—marked a fresh and satisfying departure for her. Her masterpiece is* A Head for Happy *(1931), a picture book combining elements of a mock epic, travelogue, and guessing game.*

FORWARD WITH BOOKS
BOOK WEEK
NOVEMBER 2 - 8

1942

F. HASSE
(DATES UNKNOWN)

In an earlier version of this poster, an enemy plane in flames is silhouetted in a searchlight beam. But in the final design, that incendiary touch has been eliminated, and the dour slogan "Books Will Help Us Through" has been replaced by the more upbeat "Forward with Books."

1943

Elizabeth Orton Jones
(B. 1910)

Jones was born in the Chicago suburb of Highland Park, where she enjoyed just the sort of childhood that the Book Week founders would have considered ideal. The granddaughter of a bookshop owner who was "always writing stories and plays" for children, Orton recalled that her own parents "believed in exposing their children to music, art, literature, and people of various nationalities and walks of life." Among the books for young readers she went on to illustrate are Cornelia Meigs's novel The Scarlet Oak *(1938) and Rachel Field's picture book* Prayer for a Child *(1944), for which Jones won the 1945 Caldecott Medal.*

BUILD THE FUTURE WITH BOOKS

BOOK WEEK - 1943
NOVEMBER 14ᵀᴴ-20ᵀᴴ

NEDDA WALKER
(DATES UNKNOWN)

This Canadian-born artist grew up in and around Boston and attended the Massachusetts School of Art and the Pennsylvania Academy of Fine Arts. She later specialized in portraiture and children's book illustration.

The slogan "United Through Books" expressed the cooperative spirit among librarians, booksellers, and publishers that had come to be associated with the annual Book Week observances. It also heralded the Allied Powers' plan to found a postwar United Nations. For the first time Book Week was being celebrated internationally—in England and, on a smaller scale, in Canada, Australia, New Zealand, Mexico, Nicaragua, and the Soviet Union.

1945

GERTRUDE HOWE
(B. 1902)

Howe graduated from Mount Holyoke College before going to New York City to study art at Pratt Institute and the Art Students League. She began illustrating children's books in 1926, specializing in stories featuring teenage protagonists. At the time she designed this poster, she had fifty books to her credit. Howe later tired of the freelance illustrator's often taxing routine and devoted herself to teaching and printmaking.

UNITED THROUGH BOOKS

BOOK WEEK
NOVEMBER 11-17 1945

MAUD PETERSHAM
(1889–1971) AND
MISKA PETERSHAM
(1888–1960)

During World War II, Bennett Cerf, the gregarious publisher of Random House, hosted a popular radio show called "Books Are Bullets," featuring discussions of newly published books on war-related themes. Cerf's listeners and other book-minded Americans doubtless heaved a sigh of relief on encountering the contrastingly hopeful, forward-looking "Books are Bridges" slogan of the second postwar Book Week celebration.

1947

EDGAR PARIN D'AULAIRE
(1898–1986) AND
INGRI D'AULAIRE
(1904–1980)

Edgar, the son of an Italian painter, and Ingri, the daughter of a Norwegian folklorist, were married in Europe and immigrated to the United States in 1929. The couple arrived as fine-art printmakers, but following an encounter with Anne Carroll Moore, the New York Public Library's formidable superintendent of children's work, they redirected their efforts to bookmaking for boys and girls.

Over the next forty years, the d'Aulaires' handsomely lithographed, large-format picture books and story treasuries came to epitomize the "book beautiful," intended not only to delight children but also to elevate their level of aesthetic appreciation. Ola *(1932), an early work, was one of their many picture books to feature Scandinavian settings and themes.* Abraham Lincoln, *for which the d'Aulaires received the 1940 Caldecott Medal, was one of a number of works in their Americana series.*

The heroic figures of this Book Week poster are redolent of the prewar spirit of idealism that had inspired poet Carl Sandburg, filmmaker Frank Capra, and artist Rockwell Kent to celebrate "the people."

BOOKS FOR THE WORLD OF TOMORROW

BOOK WEEK

November 16-22

BOOK WEEK
NOVEMBER 14 TO 20, 1948

BOOKS TELL THE STORY

MARGUERITE LOFFT DE ANGELI
(1889–1987)

Born in Lapeer, Michigan, de Angeli briefly considered a singing career, but chose a secure marriage instead. Then, in 1921, as a mother of three, she began to study drawing; the following year, she received her first modest commission as an illustrator from a Sunday school paper. Cornelia Meigs's The New Moon *(1924) was the first of more than a dozen books by other authors that de Angeli illustrated. In 1935, she became a published author herself with* Ted and Nina Go to the Grocery Store. *De Angeli's vigorous (if, by today's standards, sentimental) drawings made her one of America's most popular children's illustrators of the 1940s and 1950s. Her novels* Elin's Amerika *(1941) and* Bright April *(1946) were unusual for their time in their detailed and sympathetic portrayals of ethnic minorities. De Angeli received two Caldecott Honors and one Newbery Honor, and she won the 1950 Newbery Medal for* The Door in the Wall, *a novel set in 14th-century England in the reign of Edward III.*

1949

ELIZABETH TYLER WOLCOTT
(1892–1951)

In 1949, the Book Week poster artist was chosen in open competition for the first time. The winner, who had studied at Mount Holyoke and with George Grosz at the Art Students League, was the illustrator of several children's books, including James S. Tippett's popular Nursery Series of verses about modern city life. Wolcott also designed posters for various New York City welfare societies and advertising agencies and created a mural for the Brooklyn Botanic Garden.

MAKE FRIENDS WITH BOOKS

CHILDREN STORIES

BOOK WEEK

NOVEMBER 12-18, 1950

WILLIAM PÈNE DU BOIS
(1916–1993)

This poster might serve as a fitting emblem for its creator's cunning illustration art. The son of painter Guy Pène du Bois, William grew up in New York and in France. As a child, he read little, attended the circus often, and must have learned to draw: his first three picture books—Elisabeth the Cow Ghost, Giant Otto, and Otto at Sea—all appeared in 1936, when he was twenty. In a career that spanned a half century, Pène du Bois produced books marked by a dry Gallic wit, an impeccable sense of design, and an unbridled delight in absurdity. He received the 1948 Newbery Medal for The Twenty-One Balloons. For several years he served as art director of The Paris Review.

MARCIA BROWN
(B. 1918)

Born in Rochester, New York, Brown was a minister's daughter. She lived in several northeastern communities as a child and later recalled the public libraries she had found wherever her family went as one of the happy constants of those early years. After moving to New York City to study art with Stuart Davis and Yasuo Kuniyoshi, Brown worked in the Central Children's Room of the New York Public Library while completing her first four books. She soon became one of American children's literature's most honored illustrators. Between 1948 and 1954, she received an unprecedented six Caldecott Honors; in 1955, she won the first of three Caldecott Medals— also a record. Inspired by her childhood pleasure in folktales and by her storytelling experiences at the New York Public Library, Brown made a specialty of illustrating her own retellings of classic tales. Among her many titles in this vein are Stone Soup *(1947),* Cinderella *(1954), and* The Snow Queen *(1972).*

1952

ROGER DUVOISIN
(1904–1980)

In 1927, when this Swiss-born artist came to New York, he was already an accomplished designer of posters and fabrics, a potter, and an illustrator. Duvoisin further expanded his range in 1932 by writing and illustrating his first children's book, A Little Boy Was Drawing *; three years later, he made his debut as a* New Yorker *cover artist. During the 1940s, Duvoisin's droll and graceful line art was also featured in a long-running series of Lord & Taylor department store advertisements. His painterly illustrations for* White Snow, Bright Snow *by Alvin Tresselt won him the 1948 Caldecott Medal. His own picture-book series about Petunia, a goose as wise as she is silly, and* The Happy Lion *(1954) by his wife, Louise Fatio, remain favorites from the baby boom years.*

1953

JAN BALET
(B. 1913)

This German-born artist has enjoyed a many-faceted career as a children's book illustrator, commercial artist, and art director of Mademoiselle *and* Seventeen *magazines. Balet's impish urbanity is deeply rooted in the era of postwar American popular culture that produced such similarly stylish, European-flavored entertainments as* Around the World in 80 Days *and* Gigi. *His illustrations have appeared in* House Beautiful, Town & Country, Redbook, Vogue, *and* Charm, *and in advertisements for CBS, Lux, Life Savers, and the Franklin Simon and Macy's department stores. Among the children's books Balet has written and illustrated are* Ned and Ed and the Lion *(1949),* What Makes an Orchestra *(1951),* The Five Rollatinis *(1959), and* The Fence: A Mexican Tale *(1969).*

READING IS FUN

Book Week
Nov. 15-21

Lynd Ward
(1905–1985)

Ward was the son of a Methodist minister. His father's work at a Boston settlement house proved instrumental in instilling in the future artist a passionate concern for the problems of working-class people.

Ward began his professional career in 1929, when, under the influence of the Belgian graphic novelist Frans Masereel, he produced God's Man, *his first "novel in woodcuts" exploring social and spiritual questions. He entered the children's book field the following year, illustrating the first of two Newbery Medal winners, Elizabeth Coatsworth's* The Cat Who Went to Heaven. *From 1937 to 1939 Ward was director of the graphic arts division of the Federal Writers Project in New York City.*

Among the many children's books Ward illustrated are Hildegarde H. Swift's The Little Red Lighthouse and the Great Gray Bridge *(1942); the Newbery Medal winner for 1944, Esther Forbes's* Johnny Tremain; *and* The Biggest Bear, *which Ward wrote himself and for which he was awarded the 1953 Caldecott Medal.*

1955

GARTH WILLIAMS
(B. 1912)

Williams was born in New York City to British parents, both of whom were artists, and grew up in France, Canada, and England, always with some cartoon sketch or far-fetched mechanical diagram on his drawing board. While an art student in England, Williams won the coveted Prix de Rome in sculpture, and in 1941, on returning to live in the United States, he found employment at The New Yorker. *Although his association with the magazine proved short-lived (the art director considered Williams's drawing style too "polished" and "European"), his work caught the attention of staff writer E. B. White, who chose Williams to illustrate* Stuart Little *(1945).*

Williams followed that brilliant debut in the children's book field with illustrations for more than sixty other works, many of which have become classics. Among them are Margaret Wise Brown's Little Fur Family *(1946), E. B. White's* Charlotte's Web *(1952), the uniform edition of Laura Ingalls Wilder's* Little House *series (1953), Margery Sharp's* The Rescuers *(1959), George Selden's* The Cricket in Times Square *(1960), Russell Hoban's* Bedtime for Frances *(1960), and Randall Jarrell's* The Gingerbread Rabbit *(1964).*

IT'S ALWAYS BOOK TIME

BOOK WEEK, Nov. 25-Dec. 1

1956

LEONARD WEISGARD
(B. 1916)

Born in New Haven, Connecticut, Weisgard attended Pratt Institute, and quickly established himself in New York as an illustrator and commercial artist. Influenced by constructivism, the avant-garde graphics of E. McKnight Kauffer, and the cubist paintings of Stuart Davis, Weisgard was among the first American artists to introduce modernist elements of form and design to children's book illustration. Among his best-known works are his illustrations for the Noisy Book series (1939 to 1951) and The Golden Egg Book *(1947), all written by Margaret Wise Brown; for* The Little Island *by Margaret Wise Brown (writing as Golden MacDonald), for which Weisgard was awarded the 1947 Caldecott Medal; and for Alice Dalgliesh's 1955 Newbery Honor–winning* The Courage of Sarah Noble.

1957

ALICE PROVENSEN
(B. 1918) AND
MARTIN PROVENSEN
(1916–1987)

The Provensens met in the early 1940s in Hollywood, where Martin was working on Navy training films for Universal Studios and Alice was employed at the Walter Lantz Studios as an animator. In 1946, after Martin completed his military service, the couple moved east to begin their career as an illustration team. For over twenty years they published exclusively with the Golden Press and its original parent company, Simon and Schuster. Their first book, The Fireside Book of Folk Songs *(1947), edited by Margaret Bradford Boni, became a classic in its field. Among their other notable early collaborations are* The Golden Mother Goose *(1948), James A. Beard's* The Fireside Cook Book *(1949), Margaret Wise Brown's* The Color Kittens *(1949), and Jane Werner Watson's adaptation for children,* The Iliad and the Odyssey *(1956). The Provensens'* A Peaceable Kingdom: The Shaker Abecedarius *(1978) is one of the most striking American picture books of the 1970s;* The Glorious Flight: Across the Channel with Louis Blériot *won them the 1984 Caldecott Medal. Since Martin's death, Alice Provensen has embarked on a solo career.*

explore with books nov.2-8 **1958**

book week

PAUL RAND
(B. 1914)

In a career spanning a half century, Rand has distinguished himself as one of the world's foremost practitioners and teachers of graphic design. He was Esquire *magazine's art director (1936–1941); among his many corporate clients have been IBM and Westinghouse. Rand has taught at Cooper Union, Pratt Institute, and Yale; his professional writings include* Thoughts on Design *(1947) and* Design, Form, and Chaos *(1993).*

Not long after becoming parents, Rand and his wife, Ann, began collaborating on children's picture books. I Know a Lot of Things *(1956),* Sparkle and Spin *(1957),* Little 1 *(1962), and* Listen! Listen! *(1970) remain high points in the playful exploration of color, form, and type, and of collage as a childlike but sophisticated medium for picture-book art.*

1959

FEODOR ROJANKOVSKY
(1891–1970)

*Born in Mitava, Russia, Rojankovsky began
illustrating children's books during the time
of the Russian Revolution. Later, in Poland,
and then in France, he worked for fashion
magazines and publishing firms, in advertising, and in motion pictures. While in Paris,
Rojankovsky met the American expatriate
writer-publishers Esther Averill and Lila
Stanley, for whom he illustrated, among
other books, the brilliantly lithographed
picture book,* Daniel Boone *(1931). In 1941,
he moved to New York, where he illustrated
a long and impressive list of popular books,
including* The Tall Book of Mother Goose
(1942), Georges Duplaix's Gaston and
Joséphine *(1948), and John Langstaff's* Frog
Went A-Courtin', *for which he received the
1956 Caldecott Medal.*

MAURICE SENDAK
(B. 1928)

Sendak, the preeminent children's book artist of our time, was born in Brooklyn, New York, and grew up clamoring for admission to the larger, worldlier world of art, literature, and publishing. Primarily self-taught, he drew comic strips for his high school paper, received his first book commission at age nineteen, and enjoyed his first important success as the illustrator of Ruth Krauss's A Hole Is to Dig *(1952).*

By 1960 Sendak had thirty-nine books to his credit, including Meindert DeJong's The House of Sixty Fathers *(1956), Else Holmelund Minarik's* Little Bear *(1957), and his own* The Sign on Rosie's Door *(1960). Always an avid absorber of artistic styles and influences, he recalls having wanted at the time he designed this poster to draw as much as possible like illustrator André François—and perhaps also like Ben Shahn.* Where the Wild Things Are, *for which Sendak won the 1964 Caldecott Medal, gave further momentum to an extraordinary career, which has since come to encompass not only bookmaking but also design for the opera and ballet and for* The Night Kitchen, *a national children's theater, of which he is co-founder and artistic director.*

1961

PETER BURCHARD
(B. 1921)

Burchard, who was born in Washington, D.C., illustrated army training manuals during World War II. After the war, he completed his studies at the Philadelphia Museum of Art's School of Industrial Art, then went to New York, where over the next twenty years he designed book jackets and illustrated more than 100 books. Around 1970, Burchard began redirecting his efforts toward writing; since that time, he has written nearly twenty books, including historical novels for young readers and the nonfiction narrative One Gallant Rush: Robert Gould Shaw and His Brave Black Regiment *(1965), on which the 1989 movie* Glory *was based.*

I LIKE BOOKS!

Book Week   November 11-17

1962

KATE SEREDY
(1899–1975)

"I had the usual number of grandparents," this Hungarian-born author and illustrator once recalled, *"but in my case the combination was unusual because one was French, one German, one Slovakian, and one Turkish. . . . I grew up in an atmosphere charged with highly individual opinions. My collective family had in turn decided that I was to be a teacher, a nurse, a dress designer, plain wife complete with children, a thorn in the side of any government in power. . . , a painter. I have at one time or another dabbled in each career, adding occasionally a few ideas of my own."*

Seredy came to the United States in 1922, originally just for a visit. While learning English by the *"trial-and-error method,"* she earned her living painting lampshades and greeting cards, slowly *"graduating"* to fashion design, magazine and book illustration, and writing. The Good Master *(1935),* the first book Seredy both wrote and illustrated, is generally considered among her best. She had her greatest success as the author of The White Stag, *a novel about her homeland, for which she was awarded the 1938 Newbery Medal.*

1963

ADRIENNE ADAMS
(B. 1906)

Adams, who was born in Fort Smith, Arkansas, taught at a rural Oklahoma school before moving to New York in 1929. One of the first books she illustrated, Bag of Smoke *(1942), by her husband, Lonzo Anderson, tells about the Montgolfier brothers, the eighteenth-century French inventors who launched the first hot-air balloon. At a time when Americans were fascinated by the possibilities of manned space travel, Adams chose for her Book Week poster to return to an image of that earlier—but no less romantic—means of flight.*

Adams is the illustrator of dozens of children's books, including works by contemporary authors Rumer Godden and Clyde Robert Bulla, classic tales of the Brothers Grimm and Hans Christian Andersen, and several picture books of her own, among them A Woggle of Witches *(1971) and* The Easter Egg Artists *(1976).*

Three Cheers for Books!

Book Week   November 10-16, 1963

BRUNO MUNARI
(B. 1907)

Munari, who at the age of twenty briefly allied himself with the futurist movement of Italian artists, never lost his early passion for machines. Born in Milan, he has enjoyed an extraordinarily varied career as an industrial designer, photographer, painter, illustrator and designer of books, and creator of toys and mobiles.

To the children's book world, he is best known as the author-illustrator of such boldly designed works as Bruno Munari's ABC *(1960), and for a series of lift-the-flap books—including* The Elephant's Wish *(1959) and* The Birthday Present *(1959)— which raised this often mechanical novelty genre to the level of uproariously funny conceptual art.*

1965

EZRA JACK KEATS
(1916–1983)

Growing up in Brooklyn, New York, Keats counted art supplies among his most prized possessions; his mother's tablecloth was his first canvas. He attended the Art Students League, studied painting with Jean Charlot, worked as a WPA muralist, and served as a camouflage specialist during World War II. Returning to New York after the war, Keats painted, did commercial artwork, taught, and illustrated children's books. He was co-author (with Pat Cherr) and illustrator of My Dog Is Lost! *or,* ¡Mi perro se ha perdido! *(1960), a picture book that acknowledged, as few before it had, the ethnic and linguistic diversity of contemporary urban America.*

He continued experimenting in The Snowy Day *(1962), the first significant picture book in years to unselfconsciously celebrate what Keats called "the beauty and goodness of the Black child." The Snowy Day, which won the Caldecott Medal, also marked the beginning of the artist's fruitful exploration of collage, a technique that in* Whistle for Willie *(1964),* A Letter to Amy *(1968), and many later books proved well suited to capturing the kaleidoscopic diversity of urban street life.*

SING OUT FOR BOOKS

Book Week   October 31 to November 6   1965

1966

ANTONIO FRASCONI
(B. 1919)

*Frasconi was born to Italian parents in
Buenos Aires and raised in Uruguay. He
began drawing and painting while still a child,
and in 1945 he moved to New York, where
he focused increasingly on printmaking. His
fine-art woodcuts and book illustrations in
that medium have brought him international
acclaim.*

*At the invitation of an editor who was an
admirer of his prints, Frasconi created his first
work for children,* See and Say: A Picture
Book in Four Languages *(1955), a novel
experiment in multilingual bookmaking.
Frasconi later observed, "I believe that children's literature should show a broader
panorama: the diversity of other people, their
culture, their language, etc. That should be
the first step in the making of character."
The artist made* See and Say *with his own son
Pablo in mind; his Book Week poster is a
portrait of Pablo. Frasconi was awarded the
1959 Caldecott Medal for his bilingual* The
House That Jack Built.

1967

TOMI UNGERER
(B. 1931)

Ungerer grew up in Occupied France, where he recalls having experienced the terror, and peculiar excitement, of life in a war zone. A maverick by nature, he attended art school only briefly. Lured by the appeal of postwar-era American music, magazines, and literature, he went to New York in 1957, where he soon found work as a children's book artist and illustrator for Esquire, Charm, *and* Sports Illustrated *magazines. Ungerer gained a reputation as a brilliant, quick-on-the-draw imagemaker who took a devilish delight in pushing his commissioned projects right up to—and sometimes beyond—the limits of acceptable taste. His Book Week poster seems to have been based on an advertisement—featuring a human figure mounted in a catapult—that Ungerer had designed the previous year for Pepsi-Cola. The firm had thought the ad too unsettling and never used it. Among Ungerer's witty, irreverent children's books are* The Mellops Go Flying *(1957),* Crictor *(1958),* The Three Robbers *(1962), and* The Beast of Monsieur Racine *(1971). He has also designed numerous political posters, published a memoir and books of erotic drawings, and illustrated the work of others.*

GO PLACES WITH BOOKS

BOOK WEEK NOVEMBER 17–23, 1968

1968

ELLEN RASKIN
(1928–1984)

"To a child," Raskin once recalled, "the Depression was bad enough; even more painful was having to watch that dumb Shirley Temple." Raskin's pie-in-the-face sarcasm, her fascination with stories that are also puzzles or games, and her "compassion for the hurts and hazards of childhood" are some of the defining elements of a body of work that is as original as it is unusually varied. Born and raised in Milwaukee, Raskin later lived in New York, where she became a much-sought-after commercial artist, the designer of more than 1,000 book jackets and advertisements. Among the first books she illustrated are the New Directions edition of Dylan Thomas's A Child's Christmas in Wales *(1959) and Ruth Krauss's* Mama, I Wish I Was Snow, Child, You'd Be Very Cold *(1962). The best known of her own picture books,* Spectacles *(1968), gives a wryly exaggerated account of the "miraculous revelation" she experienced when, as a child, she was fitted with her first pair of glasses. Raskin is equally remembered for her longer works for older children, most notably the 1979 Newbery Medal winner,* The Westing Game.

1969

EMILY ARNOLD McCULLY
(B. 1939)

Born in Galesburg, Illinois, McCully was educated at Brown and Columbia universities. She never set out to become a children's book artist. In 1966, however, her subway poster for a New York radio station was spotted by an editor, and McCully's first book assignment soon followed. When one of the three books she illustrated in 1968, Meindert DeJong's Journey from Peppermint Street, won the National Book Award, her already growing reputation was secured.

In her design for the fiftieth anniversary Book Week poster, McCully sought to convey the "sense of empowerment that people were feeling" during the politically charged 1960s; to feature an androgynous (and thus non-sexist) central figure; and, in honor of the recent birth of her son, to include a baby. McCully was the 1993 Caldecott Medal winner for her picture book Mirette on the High Wire.

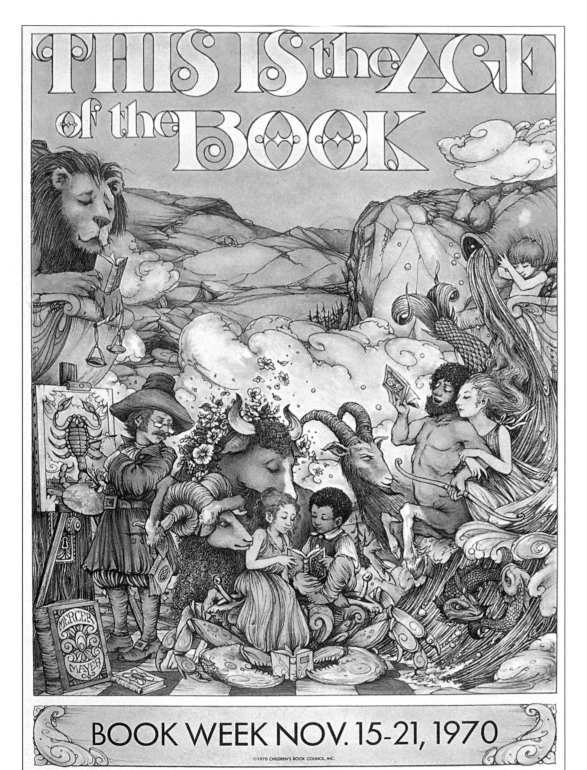

MERCER MAYER
(B. 1943)

A native of Arkansas, Mayer moved to Hawaii with his family. There he attended high school, studied art, and worked as a muralist and political cartoonist. This last experience may have had a particular bearing on his subsequent career in children's books: several of his works feature gingerly depictions of powerful, comically or grotesquely scary creatures. Among the best known are There's a Nightmare in My Closet *(1968),* Everyone Knows What a Dragon Looks Like *with text by Jay Williams (1976), and Marianna Mayer's retelling of* Beauty and the Beast *(1978).*

1971

ARNOLD LOBEL
(1933–1987)

While growing up in Schenectady, New York, Lobel made the local public library his private haven. He discovered his talent for illustration at Pratt Institute. After a stint as a commercial artist, Lobel began what he later considered his apprenticeship in the children's book field, illustrating and writing a variety of books as he gradually honed his craft. Highlights of these early years are his illustrations for Nathaniel Benchley's Red Fox and His Canoe *(1964) and his own* Martha the Movie Mouse *(1966). About 1970, his work took on a new authority and he produced memorable books of his own and in collaboration with his wife Anita Lobel and others. The Frog and Toad books, for which he won both Newbery and Caldecott Honors, are deeply felt, well-crafted contributions to the deceptively simple begin-ning-reader genre. Among his other books are* Mouse Tales *(1972), the Caldecott Medal–winning* Fables *(1980), and* The Book of Pigericks: Pig Limericks *(1983).*

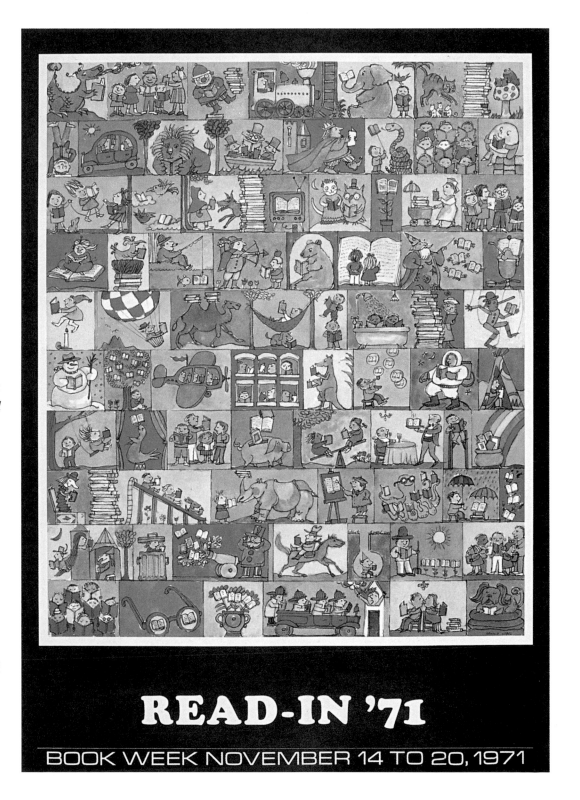

READ-IN '71

BOOK WEEK NOVEMBER 14 TO 20, 1971

BOOKS NOW!

BOOKS WOW!

BOOK WEEK · NOVEMBER 13-19, 1972

1972

WILLIAM STEIG
(B. 1907)

Steig belongs to that generation of Americans whose world view was largely shaped by their experience of the Great Depression. Born and raised in New York, the son of a housepainter and a seamstress, Steig was by nature something of a free spirit. But during the 1930s his family needed his help to pay the bills, and because he could draw, he sought work as an illustrator. The New Yorker *accepted his first cartoon when he was twenty-three, and he has been a regular contributor ever since.*

Steig was in his early sixties when he began a second career as a children's author and illustrator. His many picture books, and three longer fantasies, reveal an artist smitten in equal measure with the beauty, pathos, and absurdity of life. For the determined, good-hearted underdogs of Sylvester and the Magic Pebble *(which won the 1970 Caldecott Medal),* Doctor De Soto *(1982), and* Brave Irene *(1986), victory in life is always hard-won, and hope springs eternal.*

MARGOT ZEMACH
(1931–1989)

The daughter of a theater director and an actress, Zemach created illustrations notable for their bold-stroke dramatic energy, attention to telltale incidentals, and piquant delight in human folly. She cited Goya, Rowlandson, and Hogarth as formative influences. Among her many fine books— most of them folktales adapted by her husband, Harve Zemach—are Too Much Nose: An Italian Tale (1967); The Judge: An Untrue Tale, *a 1970 Caldecott Honor book;* A Penny Look: An Old Story Retold *(1971); and the 1974 Caldecott Medal winner,* Duffy and the Devil: A Cornish Tale Retold.

1974

JAMES MARSHALL
(1942–1992)

Marshall grew up in a Texas home filled with Hollywood glamour magazines and photographs of his pioneer forebears; outside were open fields that he imagined were the sites of the medieval battles about which he loved to read. Following high school, Marshall went to Boston to study the viola, but a hand injury ended his chances for a career in classical music. He recalled his thwarted ambition—along with a depressing marshland near his family's second Texas home—in the name he chose for one of his most memorable comic characters, Viola Swamp.

Equally a master of the outrageous put-on and the tender dramatic moment, Marshall was a self-taught artist whose seemingly guileless, devil-may-care style served to highlight those same qualities in such characters as the disarmingly gentle hippopotamus friends George and Martha, the Stupid family, and the incorrigible Fox.

Something of the artist's own mischievous nature was revealed when it became known that Edward Marshall, the author of certain books that James had illustrated, was really James himself. Marshall was one of the subtlest of writers for young readers, and his understanding of the quandaries they confront on entering the world of their peers looks to have been total.

RICHARD SCARRY
(B. 1919–1994)

Scarry grew up in Boston, where his family owned a small chain of department stores. After proving himself less than devoted academically, he enrolled at the School of the Museum of Fine Arts, Boston, where he began to come into his own. Following wartime military service, Scarry went to New York, planning on a career in commercial art. But in 1949 he landed an assignment to illustrate a book for the Golden Press, and was thereafter never without work as an illustrator of children's picture books.

His first major commercial success, Richard Scarry's Best Word Book Ever (1963), established a niche for him as a maker of copiously illustrated picture books surveying real-world phenomena—the animal kingdom, modes of human transportation—with broad humor and in satisfying detail. Scarry was the author and illustrator of nearly 130 books in all. His work has been translated into twenty-eight languages.

BOOKMAGIC

BOOK WEEK / NOVEMBER 8-14, 1976

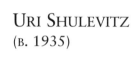

1976

URI SHULEVITZ
(B. 1935)

Shulevitz was born in Warsaw and lived in Paris and Israel before arriving in New York. His first book, The Moon in My Room *(1963), has been followed by more than twenty-five others, including* One Monday Morning *(1967),* Rain Rain Rivers *(1969),* The Fool of the World and the Flying Ship, *for which he was awarded the 1969 Caldecott Medal,* The Treasure, *a 1980 Caldecott Honor book, and* The Secret Room *(1993). Shulevitz has also taught picture-book workshops and is the author of the widely read text* Writing with Pictures *(1985).*

Shulevitz's poster illustration is a clever allegory on the year's theme. In it, elements of reality (a cityscape, a cat) and fantasy (a flying figure, a storybook scene that can literally be entered) are seamlessly joined through the "magic" of reading.

ANITA LOBEL
(B. 1934)

"Browsing in the bookstalls along the Seine in the spring of 1975," Anita Lobel has recalled, *"I came upon some reproductions of seventeenth-century trade posters. The engravings depict monumental figures of tradespeople extravagantly costumed in the products and implements of their occupations."* Inspired by these Baroque fantasies, Lobel designed the poster shown here, and went on to create a gallery of such fanciful characters for the alphabet book On Market Street, *with text by Arnold Lobel, for which she received a 1982 Caldecott Honor.*

Born in Cracow, Lobel was still a child when she fled Nazi-occupied Poland and was later imprisoned in a German concentration camp. After the war, she lived in Sweden before coming to the United States in 1952. In New York, she attended Pratt Institute, pursued an interest in the theater, met her future husband and collaborator, Arnold Lobel, and worked as a textile designer. Her first picture book, Sven's Bridge (1965), *was published to considerable fanfare. Besides Arnold Lobel, her collaborators have included Meindert DeJong, Alice Dalgliesh, Mirra Ginsburg, John Langstaff, and Charlotte S. Huck.*

BOOK WEEK
Nov. 14-20, 1977 *Read All About It*

© 1977 The Children's Book Council, Inc.

Laurent de Brunhoff

HELLO BOOK

Book Week~Nov. 13-19 1978

LAURENT DE BRUNHOFF
(B. 1925)

This picture-book artist inherited from his father, Jean, not only a talent for drawing and an elegant, wry sense of design but also a well-loved cast of characters—Babar, King of the Elephants, his family and friends—several of whom are depicted here.

Born in Paris, de Brunhoff grew up in heady cultural surroundings. His grandfather and three uncles were the publishers or editors of important French art and fashion magazines. His mother, Cécile, was a pianist; it was in the bedtime stories she told Laurent and his younger brother Mathieu that Babar the elephant hero was born. From that casual beginning, Jean created The Story of Babar *(1931) and six other picture books before his untimely death in 1937 at the age of thirty-seven.*

Laurent, who was then twelve, went on to study painting, experimenting with abstraction before deciding to continue the work of his father. Laurent's first children's book, Babar's Cousin: That Rascal Arthur *(1947), has been followed by more than forty others, the majority of which feature the gentle, doughty elephant and his world.*

1979

ROSEMARY WELLS
(B. 1943)

Wells was born in New York City, studied at the School of the Museum of Fine Arts, Boston, and served her apprenticeship as an art editor for Allyn and Bacon and as a book designer for Macmillan. Wells traces her understanding of story structure and comic timing to her familiarity with musical theater, poetry, and drama, and to the routines of TV comedians like Sid Caesar and Imogene Coca. Her first published work, A Song to Sing, O! (1968), was based on a song from a Gilbert and Sullivan operetta.

Wells is the author and illustrator of a popular series of board books and picture books about the growing pains and domestic adventures of two rabbit siblings, Max and Ruby, as well as of such other picture-book standards as Morris's Disappearing Bag (1975) and Shy Charles (1988). She is also the illustrator of books by Lore Segal, Susan Jeffers, and Paula Fox, and the author of several young adult novels.

CHILDREN'S·BOOK·WEEK·NOVEMBER 17–23·1980

©1980 The Children's Book Council, Inc.

TRINA SCHART HYMAN
(B. 1939)

As a pre-schooler, this artist taught herself to read by puzzling out the words of "Little Red Riding Hood," her favorite childhood story. Hyman studied art in Philadelphia, Boston, and Stockholm and became a professional illustrator in the early 1960s. For several years beginning in 1972, she was also art director of Cricket *magazine. Among the books by others that she has illustrated are Ruth Sawyer's* Joy to the World *(1966), Eleanor Cameron's* A Room Made of Windows *(1971), and Jean Fritz's* Will You Sign Here, John Hancock? *(1976). Her own retelling of* Little Red Riding Hood *was a 1984 Caldecott Honor book; the following year, she won the Caldecott Medal for* Saint George and the Dragon.

1981

WENDY WATSON
(B. 1942)

Born in Paterson, New Jersey, Watson grew up in Vermont in a large family of artists and writers. After studying Classics at Bryn Mawr, she took painting and drawing classes on Cape Cod and at the National Academy of Design in New York. She began illustrating books in the mid-1960s. Watson is the author-illustrator of a dozen children's books and the illustrator of more than sixty others, including Father Fox's Pennyrhymes (1971), with text by her sister Clyde Watson, John Bierhorst's Doctor Coyote (1987), her own Tales for a Winter's Eve (1988), and Wendy Watson's Mother Goose (1989).

Get Lost in a Book

BOOK WEEK · NOVEMBER 15–21, 1982

JAMES STEVENSON
(B. 1929)

This prolific artist and author, who grew up in upstate New York and studied at Yale, worked as a Life *reporter during the mid-1950s before joining the staff of* The New Yorker. *For many years he wrote unsigned "Talk of the Town" pieces while producing gently satirical cartoons for the magazine in his darting, elegant, will-o'-the-wisp style and, in his spare time, writing novels. Stevenson's career in children's books began in the late 1960s, when he invited his eight-year-old son, James, to invent a story for him to illustrate; the resulting collaboration was published as* If I Owned a Candy Factory *(1968). Subsequent collaborators have included Charlotte Zolotow, Jack Prelutsky, Alan Arkin, Else Holmelund Minarik, and Dr. Seuss. Stevenson is also the illustrator of numerous picture books of his own, including* Yuck! *(1984) and the autobiographical* Higher on the Door *(1987).*

1983

TOMIE dePAOLA
(B. 1934)

DePaola was born and raised in Meriden, Connecticut, where, by the age of four, he had decided to become a writer and illustrator. He studied art at Pratt Institute and at the California College of Arts and Crafts, and has illustrated nearly 200 books, a third of which he also wrote. Among his many popular works are Strega Nona, *for which he was awarded a 1976 Caldecott Honor,* The Clown of God *(1978),* The Story of the Three Wise Kings *(1983), Jean Fritz's* Shh! We're Writing the Constitution *(1987), and the autobiographical* Tom *(1993).*

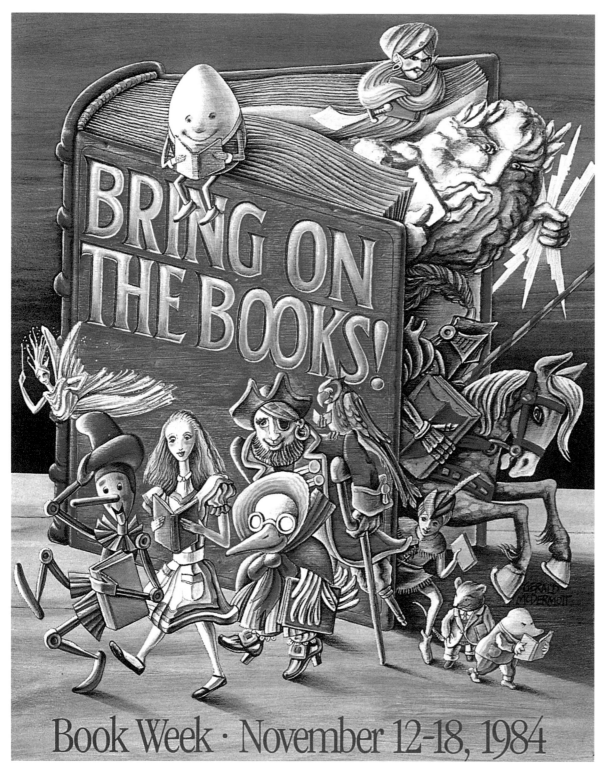

Book Week · November 12-18, 1984

GERALD McDERMOTT
(B. 1941)

At the age of four, McDermott was enrolled in a children's program at the Detroit Institute of Art that laid the groundwork for his lifelong fascination with artmaking and mythology. Between the ages of nine and eleven, he was regularly heard on a local radio program that featured dramatizations of folktales and legends. Subsequent training at a Bauhaus-inspired technical high school and at New York's Pratt Institute led him to concentrate on making animated films based on traditional story material. Early in his film career, an encounter with mythologist Joseph Campbell confirmed him in his choice of artistic direction.

In the 1960s McDermott became interested in retelling mythic tales in the picture-book format as well. His first children's book, Anansi the Spider, *was a 1973 Caldecott Honor winner and was followed by* Arrow to the Sun, *the 1975 Caldecott Medal book,* Papagayo, the Mischief Maker *(1980),* Zomo the Rabbit *(1992), and* Raven, *which received a 1993 Caldecott Honor.*

1985

MARC BROWN
(B. 1946)

Childhood visits to the Art Institute of Chicago and the early encouragement of his grandmother inspired Brown to become an artist. As a painting major at the Cleveland Institute of Art, he experimented with children's book illustration, but, as was typical at the time, his instructors and contemporaries dismissed his efforts in that vein as a downward step on the ladder of "serious" artmaking. After teaching and working as a textbook illustrator, Brown secured his first children's book assignment, illustrating Isaac Asimov's What Makes the Sun Shine? *(1971). He has since created the art for a long list of books by Peter Dickinson, Diane Wolkstein, Verna Aardema, Jack Prelutsky, and his wife, Laurene Krasny Brown, and has written and illustrated many picture books of his own, including the Arthur the aardvark adventure series.*

REACH FOR A BOOK

BOOK WEEK · NOVEMBER · 17-23

© 1986 The Children's Book Council, Inc.

1986

CHRIS VAN ALLSBURG
(B. 1949)

As a child who loved to draw, this artist favored subjects like the fumbling comic-strip character Dagwood Bumstead. As a student at the University of Michigan and the Rhode Island School of Design, Van Allsburg became interested in sculpture, and his work began to develop a surrealistic edge. A tendency to produce art with an element of implied narrative led him to experiment, tentatively, with illustration. Van Allsburg's first published work, The Garden of Abdul Gasazi, won a 1980 Caldecott Honor and immediately established him as a picture-book artist of the first rank. Jumanji, his next book, was the 1982 Caldecott Medal winner and was followed by such strikingly original works as The Mysteries of Harris Burdick (1984) and the perennial holiday favorite The Polar Express, for which he won a second Caldecott Medal in 1986.

MARC SIMONT
(B. 1915)

The son of a draftsman for the legendary French weekly L'Illustration, *Simont was born in Paris and traveled widely before settling permanently in the United States. An early friend in his adoptive country was another aspiring young illustrator, Robert McCloskey; for a time Simont shared the Greenwich Village apartment in which McCloskey kept a flock of live birds while completing the illustrations for* Make Way for Ducklings *(1941). A portrait painter, caricaturist, and onetime artist for* Sports Illustrated, *Simont has illustrated children's books for more than fifty years. His vast and distinguished body of work in the children's field includes collaborations with James Thurber, Margaret Wise Brown, Ruth Krauss, Faith McNulty, Meindert DeJong, David McCord, and Karla Kuskin. In 1957, he received the Caldecott Medal for Janice May Udry's* A Tree Is Nice.

BOOK WEEK · November 16-22, 1987

WISH UPON A BOOK

BOOK WEEK★NOVEMBER 14-20, 1988

STEVEN KELLOGG
(B. 1941)

While growing up in suburban Norwalk, Connecticut, Kellogg liked to pretend he was a staff artist for National Geographic *and dream up assignments that allowed him to pursue his passion for animal illustration. Ever since then, animals have figured prominently in his art. Kellogg has illustrated over seventy-five picture books and is the author of more than twenty. His popular work has often been honored for its broad humor, unflagging good cheer, and generosity of spirit.*

RICHARD EGIELSKI
(B. 1952)

It seems only natural that Egielski, as a child of the 1950s, would have developed his passion for drawing in part from watching TV—Jon Gnagy's popular Learn to Draw *series and cartoons like* Betty Boop *and* Popeye. *Egielski attended New York's High School of Art and Design and discovered the picture book a few years later, in a seminar taught by Maurice Sendak at the Parsons School of Design. His first published work,* Sid and Sol *(1977), was a major critical success for both him and for his first-time author-collaborator, Arthur Yorinks. Yorinks's streetwise, stand-up-comic style of delivery meshed well with Egielski's distinctive brand of visual slapstick. Subsequent collaborations with Yorinks include* Louis the Fish *(1980) and the 1987 Caldecott Medal book,* Hey, Al. *This poster is a reprise of the Caldecott winner, featuring Al and a few of his furry and feathery friends.*

ED YOUNG
(B. 1931)

Young was born in Tientsin, China, grew up in Shanghai, and lived in Hong Kong before coming to the United States on a student visa. On graduating from the Los Angeles Art Center, he went to New York to look for work as a commercial artist. A longing for more satisfying forms of artistic expression led him during the 1960s, however, to try his hand at picture-book art. To Young, that genre seemed related to traditional Chinese painting, in which words are often combined with an image. His many books reveal a playful but disciplined poetic sensibility. By incorporating such traditional Chinese elements as the paper cut and calligraphy, Young has enlarged the picture book's visual vocabulary. Lon Po Po: A Red-Riding Hood Story from China *brought Young the 1990 Caldecott Medal.*

1991

PAUL O. ZELINSKY
(B. 1953)

Zelinsky, who was born in Evanston, Illinois, studied children's book illustration with Maurice Sendak at Yale and painting at Philadelphia's Tyler Institute. Among the many books he has illustrated are The Maid and the Mouse and the Odd-Shaped House *(1981);* Rika Lesser's retelling of Hanscl and Gretel *(1984), a Caldecott Honor book;* Rumpelstiltskin *(1986), also a Caldecott Honor winner;* The Wheels on the Bus *(1990); and the Carl Sandburg story collection* More Rootabagas *(1993).*

Zelinsky's quirky wit, his fascination with trompe l'oeil, and his powerful gift for representational realism are all on display in this accomplished poster, which is also a portrait of his two daughters, Anna and Rachel.

READ THINK DREAM

BOOK WEEK
NOVEMBER 16-22 1992

Fred Marcellino

FRED MARCELLINO
(B. 1939)

As a child in New York City, this illustrator and graphic artist read comic books and adored Disney cartoons. As a high school student, he steeped himself in the paintings of Van Gogh and Gauguin and the music of Ravel and Tchaikovsky, and had the benefit of an inspired teacher who pointed him toward a career in art. After studies at Cooper Union, Yale, and in Italy on a Fulbright grant, Marcellino freelanced in New York as an editorial illustrator and designer of record album covers.

He first came to prominence, however, as the designer of several strikingly effective book jackets, including those for Tom Wolfe's The Bonfire of the Vanities, *Margaret Atwood's* The Handmaid's Tale, *and Anne Tyler's* The Accidental Tourist. *Marcellino's first artistic venture into a book's interior came with his black-and-white pencil illustrations for Tor Seidler's* A Rat's Tale *(1986). He has since illustrated two picture books based on classic stories:* Puss in Boots, *for which he was awarded a 1991 Caldecott Honor, and* The Steadfast Tin Soldier *(1992); and a second fantasy by Tor Seidler,* The Wainscot Weasel.

1993

WILLIAM JOYCE
(B. 1957)

A fascination with the icons and artifacts of American popular culture informs this deftly amusing illustrator's idiosyncratic, retro approach to picture-book art. A lifelong resident of Shreveport, Louisiana, Joyce began drawing while in grade school. He studied filmmaking and illustration at Southern Methodist University, securing his first professional work as a book illustrator while still an undergraduate. Among the picture books Joyce has both written and illustrated are George Shrinks (1985), Dinosaur Bob (1988), and Bently & Egg (1992). The deadpan image featured here of friendly, book-bearing aliens recalls a similar scene from another Joyce picture book, A Day with Wilbur Robinson (1990), in which, when the Robinson family's Uncle Art arrives for a visit by flying saucer, not one of the good-natured, oddball Robinson clan is the least bit fazed.

BOOK WEEK NOVEMBER 14-20, 1994

BOOKS FOR EVERYONE
EVERYONE FOR BOOKS

1994

JERRY PINKNEY
(B. 1939)

Pinkney was born in Philadelphia and studied illustration and design at the Philadelphia College of Art. A highly versatile artist, he designed a set of commemorative stamps for the United States Postal Service's Black Heritage Series (1983) and served on the NASA artist team for the space shuttle Columbia. He has illustrated calendars, textbooks, a series of limited-edition books for collectors published by the Franklin Library, and more than sixty children's books. Pinkney's illustrations for Patricia C. McKissack's Mirandy and Brother Wind (1988) earned him the first of two Caldecott Honors. His collaborators in the children's book field have also included Verna Aardema, Virginia Hamilton, Julius Lester, Eloise Greenfield, Jean Marzollo, and his wife, Gloria Jean Pinkney.

Index of Illustrators

Index of Slogans